Disclaimer: All answers are correct as of 25th August 2021.

Stenlake Publications presents:

Spurs Crossword

Check out our other books:

Liverpool Crossword
Manchester United Crossword
Arsenal Crossword
Chelsea Crossword
Manchester City Crossword
Leeds United Crossword
Newcastle United Crossword
Sunderland Crossword
Leicester City crossword
Celtic Crossword
Rangers Crossword
England Crossword

"Bill (Nicholson) eventually became Mr Tottenham Hotspur. and produced such a dazzling team at White Hart Lane that they won the double and played the game in a way that was an object lesson to everybody".

- Brian Clough

" Its been my life. Tottenham Hotspur. and I love the club."

- Bill Nicholson

"The great fallacy is that the game is first and last about winning. It is nothing of the kind. The game is about glory. it is about doing things in style and with a flourish. about going out and beating the lot. not waiting for them to die of boredom."

- Danny Blanchflower

Contents Page

Tottenham Hotspur Football Club were founded in 1882 after a group of schoolboys from the local cricket club wanted a sport to play in the winter months. The club turned professional in 1895 and have gone on to become one of the biggest clubs in the world. This crossword covers the earliest decades of the club's history.

Across

6. The club was founded as _____ Football Club.

7. The club's first ever manager. (5,8)

10. Spurs were controversially overlooked for a spot in the expanded 1919 First Division which instead went to this side. sparking a fierce rivalry that lasts to this day.

12. Nursery club established in 1922. formalised in 1931 and lasted until WWII that produced 37 Spurs players.

14. Midlands club defeated in the 1921 FA Cup Final. (13.9)

15. Spurs became the first and still only non-league club to win the FA Cup since the Football League began having beaten this Yorkshire side in the 1901 Final. (9.6)

16. The only player to make 400 appearances and score 100 goals for Spurs and scored the winner in the 1921 FA Cup Final. (5.7)

17. One-club man who managed the club from 1949-55 who won back-to-back League titles by consecutively winning the Second and First Division title and is credited with inventing the "one-two". (6.4)

18. Spurs' initial shirts were this colour. (4.4)

19. Scored 138 goals in 198 appearances for Spurs before becoming the first player since 1906 to move directly between Spurs and Arsenal when he did so in 1937. (6.4)

Down

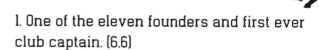

1. One of the eleven founders and first ever club captain. (6.6)

2. Spurs were eventually elected to the Football League after this Staffordshire side resigned. (5.4)

3. The club signed their first ever international player when they signed this Welshman in 1897 (also the name of a modern clothing brand). (4.5)

4. Ground that they moved into in 1899. (5.4.4)

5. Spurs wore blue and white halved shirts between 1884-89 inspired by this Lancashire club. (9.6)

7. The Payne Boots Affair involved the player Ernie Payne who played for this fellow London club.

8. Manager who led Spurs to their first FA Cup. (4.7)

9. Key signing made in 1949 who would go on to win the 1966 World Cup with England as manager. (3.6)

11. Chairman from 1899-1943. (7.7)

13. Goalkeeper who made 452 appearances for the club between 1946-58. (3.9)

Round 2 - 1950/60s

The most successful time for the club in which Spurs became champions of England for the first time by securing the title in 1951 and followed it up with their second 10 years later. They became the first team in the 20th century to win the double. doing so in 1960/61. They added two further FA Cups and a European Cup Winners' Cup in this period.

Across

1. Inside forward tragically killed by a lightning strike at the age of 27 in 1964. (4.5)

4. Forward signed for a club-record £125,000 from Southampton making him the most expensive player in the country at the time. (6.7)

5. Spurs' start to the 1960/61 season of 11 wins in a row and 16 games unbeaten was the best in the top flight until this side beat it in 2017. (10.4)

6. Spurs' third record goalscorer having netted 208 goals in 317 matches. (5.5)

7. Lancashire side defeated in the 1962 FA Cup Final.

8. Welsh winger signed from Swansea in 1958 who went on to score 159 goals in 378 appearances. (5.5)

11. Guernsey-born player nicknamed "The Duke" who scored 134 goals in 307 appearances. (3.8)

13. Spurs secured the 1960/61 league title by beating this Yorkshire side with three games to go who were also the eventual runners up. (9.9)

14. Midlands side that Spurs beat in the 1961 FA Cup Final to become the first side to do the double in the 20th century. (9.4)

17. The highest scoring FA Cup tie in the 20th Century and Spurs' record win of 13-2 came against this Cheshire side in 1959. (5.9)

18. London side beaten in the 1967 FA Cup Final.

19. The only non-Englishman in Spurs' top 10 appearances list. signed from Dundee in 1964. (4.7)

20. Scotsman known as "the heartbeat" of Spurs' most successful side and praised by George Best as the hardest and bravest opponent he ever faced. (4.6)

Down

2. Chelsea club legend signed in 1965 who punched Dave Mackay during an early training session. (5.8)

3. Two-time winner of the FWA Footballer of the Year whilst at Spurs having signed from Aston Villa in 1954. (5.12)

9. Had a 36-year association with Spurs including 16 as manager between 1958-74. (4.9)

10. Player signed for £99.999 in 1961 who would go on to become the club's all-time leading goalscorer. (5.7)

12. Spurs became the first British side to win a European Trophy when they beat this Spanish side in the 1963 European Cup Winners' Cup Final. (8.6)

15. Scored a 25-yarder in the 1963 Cup Winners' Cup Final. (5.5)

16. Tactic used by Arthur Rowe in the 1950s which later became dubbed the "Spurs Way". (4.3.3)

After some success in the early 70s including a first and second League Cup. there was. however. a period of decline for the club including a relegation in 1977. Nonetheless. the team bounced back and in the 80s. Spurs won back-to-back FA Cups as well as the UEFA Cup in 1984.

Across

3. All-time record appearance holder whose Spurs career spanned three decades. (5,8)

5. Substitute who scored the only goal for Spurs as they retained the League Cup in 1973. (5,6)

8. World Cup winner signed from West Ham in 1970 with Jimmy Greaves going the other way. (6,6)

11. English side defeated in the first ever UEFA Cup Final in 1972. (13,9)

13. Manager appointed from Luton Town in 1986 who played with what was for that time an unusual five-man midfield formation. (5,5)

16. Chairman who made Spurs the first club to be floated in the London Stock Exchange transformed English football clubs into business ventures. (6,7)

17. Scored a headed goal in his last appearance for the club in the 1972 UEFA Cup Final. (4,7)

18. Club that Glenn Hoddle was sold to in 1987.

19. Argentina World Cup winner signed in 1978. (5,7)

20. Scored a club-record 49 goals in all competitions in the 1986/87 season. (5,5)

Down

1. England international striker signed from Barcelona for £1.2 million in 1989.

2. Player who Spurs paid a national record fee of £2 million to Newcastle for in 1988. (4,9)

4. Saved a penalty in the 1984 UEFA Cup Final against Anderlecht in the shoot-out. (4,4)

6. Manager who won three major trophies with Spurs in his 7 seasons at the club. (5,10)

7. Former Arsenal player appointed manager in 1974. (5,4)

9. Northern Irish goalkeeper who was controversially sold to Arsenal for a mere £45,000 in 1977. (3,8)

10. Side they beat in the 1971 League Cup Final to secure the trophy for the first time. (5,5)

12. Aberdeen manager who reportedly reneged on an agreement to take over in 1984. (4,8)

14. Club legend attacking midfielder who netted 110 goals in 490 games. (5,6)

15. Scored a memorable winning goal against Man City in the 100th FA Cup Final. (5,5)

The 90s were a difficult period for the club as they suffered from financial troubles. They regularly finished mid table in the league. however. there was another FA Cup added in 1991 and League Cup in 1999.

Across

3. Became the first player to win the PFA Players' Player of the Year and FWA Footballer of the Year whilst playing for a club outside the top four. (5.6)

5. Scored a memorable 30-yard free-kick in a 1990/91 FA Cup semi-final against Arsenal. (4.9)

6. Fan favourite David Ginola scored a memorable goal in an FA Cup sixth round tie against this Yorkshire club.

9. Former player appointed manager in 1993 who would deploy a five-striker formation not seen in English football since the 1950s. 5.7)

13. Spurs became the first side to win eight FA Cups when they defeated this side in the 1991 Final. (10.6)

15. Scored a dramatic 93rd minute diving header to win the 1999 League Cup. (5.7)

16. Apprentice star who came in as Chairman and part-owner in 1991 and proved to be a controversial figure among Spurs fans (4.5)

17. Gerry Francis spurned the chance to sign this young Dutchman who was a fan of Glenn Hoddle and would eventually join Arsenal. (6.8)

18. Opponents in the 1999 League Cup Final victory. (9.4)

19. Arsenal legend appointed manager in 1998 to the dismay of many Spurs fans. (6.6)

Down

1. Asian nation that Gary Lineker left Spurs to play in.

2. Club record signing made in 1992 from Nottingham Forest that was subject of allegations of "bungs" against Forest manager Brian Clough. (5.10)

4. German striker signed in 1994. (6.9)

7. Newcastle striker signed as a replacement for Teddy Sheringham after his move to Manchester United. (3.9)

8. Belgium-born Wales international nicknamed "Psycho Pat". (3.3.3.5)

10. Swiss who was surprisingly appointed manager for the 1997/98 season but failed to make an impact. (9.5)

11. Midfielder signed from Borussia Dortmund in 1998 who became a fan favourite despite failing to find the net in his 131 appearances for the club. (7.6)

12. 1994 summer signings Ilie Dumitrescu and Gheorghe Popescu were from this nation.

14. 1994/95 Premier League winning captain signed in 1999 who would later go on to manage the club. (3.8)

18. Gascoigne became a transfer target for this Italian team, however, his transfer was delayed a year after he aggravated an injury on a night out.

The 2000s saw a range of positions from a low of 14th to a high of 4th and a sole trophy with the 2008 League Cup. Despite a lack of trophies, the club consistently qualified for Europe having done so in all but one season since 2006 after just two appearances in the previous 14 seasons before that.

Across

1. Scored 5 goals in a 9-1 thrashing of Wigan Athletic in 2009. (7.5)

4. Spurs got pipped to a top 4 spot on the final day of the 2005/06 season after defeat against this side with most of the side out due to food poisoning. (4.3.6)

6. Club captain who joined arch rivals Arsenal on a Bosman in one of the most stunning transfers in English football history. (3.8)

9. Frenchman appointed in 2004 who would become Spurs shortest serving manager having quit after just 13 games. (7.7)

10. Scored the winner and received man of the match in the 2008 League Cup Final. (8.8)

17. Player scored after 10 seconds against Bradford in 2000. the quickest goal in Premier League history until 2018. (6.4)

18. 2005 signing who often stood out on the football field due to his dreadlocked hair and the protective goggles he wore due to glaucoma. (5.6)

19. Uruguayan signed from Chelsea who'd go on to make 98 appearances and score 23 goals. (3.5)

20. Appointed chairman in 2001 after Alan Sugar sold his shares in the club after a sale to ENIC International Ltd. (6.4)

Down

2. Player signed for £10.6 million from Bayer Leverkusen. (7.8)

3. Juande Ramos' first signing as Spurs manager for a club record equalling £16.5 million. (4.6)

5. Ukrainian striker signed for a club record £11 million from Dynamo Kiev in 2000. (6.6)

7. Opponents in the 2008 League Cup Final.

8. The Republic of Ireland's record appearance holder and goalscorer who scored 122 goals across two spells for Spurs. (6.5)

11. Manager appointed in 2008 who would later lead Spurs to their first ever Champions League campaign in it's new format. (5.8)

12. Scored a stunning volley at former club Arsenal in a 4-4 draw in 2008. (5.7)

13. Side that Dimitar Berbatov scored a hat trick against in a 6-4 Premier League win in 2007.

14. Club that Welshman Gareth Bale was signed from.

15. Dutchman promoted from assistant manager and led Spurs to back-to-back fifth place finishes. their highest in 16 years. (6.3)

16. Top scorer in the 2008/09 season. (6.4)

Round 6 - 2010s

The club broke into the traditional "big 4" and were able to consistently qualify for the Champions League and compete for trophies. The 2016/17 season provided a club Premier League record 86 points. a highest league position since 1963 and finished above Arsenal for the first time in 22 years. Spurs also reached their first ever European Cup/Champions League Final in 2019.

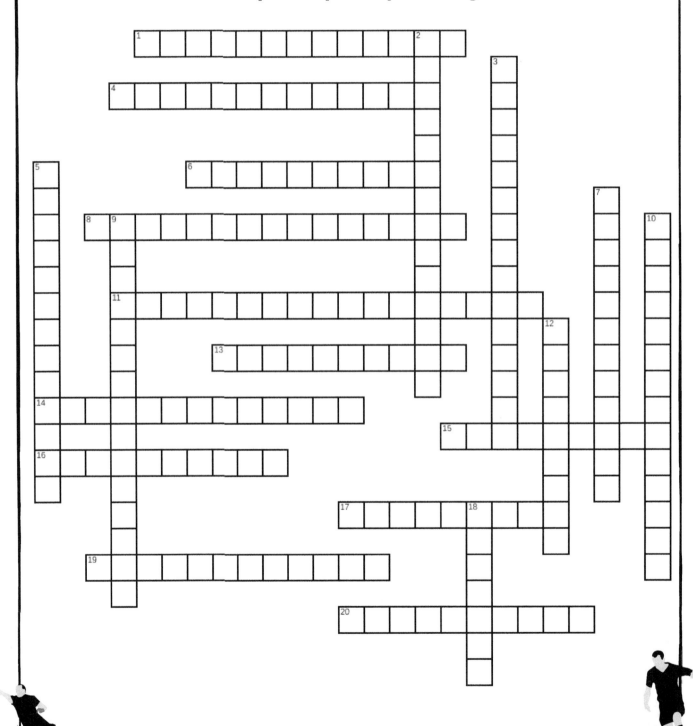

Across

1. Side who Spurs beat 5-4 on the final day of the 2017/18 season. (9,4)

4. First Kenyan to play for the club. (6,7)

6. Player who left for a world record fee. (6,4)

8. Spurs' record attendance of 85,612 came in a 2017 Champions League match against this side. (5,10)

11. Dutchman who became a professional darts player after retiring from football. (6,3,3,5)

13. Scored a hat-trick in the Champions League semi-final against Ajax to overturn a 3-0 deficit. (5,5)

14. Spurs' second place finish and 86 points tally in 2016/17 was the highest in 54 years since this manager was in charge. (4,9)

15. Scored a stunning volley on his Spurs debut against Arsenal in 2010. (5,4)

16. Scored a stunning 25-yarder against Liverpool at White Hart Lane in 2011. (4,6)

17. Academy graduate who made 70 appearances for the club before being sold to Hull City for £13 million. (4,5)

19. England and Manchester United legend who spent time in Spurs' youth academy and trained briefly with the first team in 2011. (5,7)

20. Became the first Spurs player since Jimmy Greaves to win the World Cup whilst playing for Spurs. (4,6)

Down

2. Spurs' record away win of 7-0 came in 2019 against this side in an FA Cup tie. (8,6)

3. Spurs pipped Liverpool to the signing of this Hoffenheim midfielder in 2012. (5,10)

5. £55 million club record signing made in 2019. (6,7)

7. Scored an 86th winner against Arsenal to secure Spurs' first win at Arsenal since 1993. (6,6)

9. Manager who succeeded Harry Redknapp. (5,6,4)

10. Man City player whose injury time goal was ruled out by VAR in the 2018/19 Champions League quarter-final second leg. (6,8)

12. Has been top goalscorer every season since 2014/15. (5,4)

18. Side who Spurs beat in the 2010/11 Champions League round of 16. (2,5)

Round 7 - Bill Nicholson

⊛ Bill Nicholson is the most important figure in the club's history having spent 36 years at the club. As a player he won the First Division in 1950/51 and went on to win eight major trophies in his 16 years as manager including the double in 1960/61 as well as the club's first European trophy in 1963.

Across

3. He coached the football team of this prestigious university whilst he was a player.

7. Club he made 19 guest appearances for whilst working in the Durham Light Infantry during WWII.

9. Sports historian and author who wrote biographies on Nicholson and Danny Blanchflower. (6,6)

10. Manager whose first request at Spurs was to bring back Nicholson as a consultant in 1976. (5,10)

11. He was assistant to this England manager at the 1958 World Cup. (6,12)

14. A testimonial match was played in Nicholson's honour in 2001 against this Italian side.

15. Manager who preceded him at Spurs. (5,8)

16. Northern county he was born in.

17. He was part of the England squad for the 1950 World Cup which was hosted in this nation.

18. Type 1 diabetic who Nicholson scouted from Bristol Rovers that went on to make 619 appearances for the club. (4,7)

19. Defender who Nicholson scouted from Weymouth who would go on to make over 200 appearances including captaining the 1984 UEFA Cup Final. (6,7)

Down

1. Scottish goalkeeper signed by Nicholson in 1959 who would go on to make 222 league appearances for Spurs. (4,5)

2. Nicholson narrowly missed out on qualifying for the club's first ever European Cup Final after they lost to this Portuguese side in the semis.

4. Manager he won the 1951 First Division under. (6,4)

5. London club he spent a year as advisor and scout after leaving Spurs. (4,3,6)

6. Lancashire side he made his Spurs debut against in 1938. (9,6)

7. Spurs' nursery club where Nicholson learned his trade as a player. (10,6)

8. Nicholson scored with his first touch on his only England cap against Portugal in 1951 hosted at this stadium. (8,4)

12. Nicholson was appalled by the hooliganism he witnessed in the 1974 UEFA Cup Final against this side which contributed to his disillusionment with football.

13. Nicholson's England career was a short one due to his club before country mentality and the dominance of this Wolves legend in his position who he admitted was the better player. (5,6)

Round 8 - Managers

Spurs have had over 40 managers (including caretakers) in their history with varying degrees of success. Here are 20 clues to help you fill in this crossword

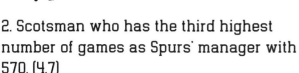

Across

2. Scotsman who has the third highest number of games as Spurs' manager with 570. (4.7)

4. Club legend who took over as caretaker in 1994. (5.8)

5. Named European coach of the year in 2007 and took charge of Real Madrid after his stint at Spurs. (6.5)

7. Resigned from the French national team just before Euro 2004 to take charge of Spurs. (7.7)

9. Had two War-interrupted spells as boss and is the first man to win the FA Cup as a player and manager. (5.9)

11. Spurs' first foreign manager. (5.7)

13. Former player who took over as caretaker manager in 2021 at the age of 29. (4.5)

14. Achieved a highest league position in 54 years since 1962-63 and led Spurs to their first ever Champions League Final. (8.10)

16. Manager who, in his only full season, finished third in Division One, reached the FA Cup Final and League Cup semi-final but was dismissed due to disclosures about his private life. (5.5)

17. The first to be sacked by Daniel Levy. (6.6)

18. Became only the second Spurs manager to win his first two North London derbies. (4.8)

19. Manager who led England to the 1998 World Cup before becoming Spurs' manager in 2001. (5.6)

20. Manager from 1984-86 and 1991-92. (5.8)

Down

1. Last manager to win the FA Cup with Spurs. (5.8)

3. The first manager since Keith Burkinshaw to qualify for European football in successive seasons. (6.3)

6. Became the first Tottenham manager to win at Old Trafford in 23 years after his side beat Manchester United 2-3. (5.6.4)

8. Manager in between legends Rowe and Nicholson who some saw as a stop gap to allow Bill to develop further as a coach. (5.8)

10. Became only the second manager to win the Premier League Manager of the Year having not won the title. (5.8)

12. The tabloid ridicule of this manager was often linked to his poor grasp of English and first Spurs press conference, where he arrived late from Heathrow Airport brandishing a London Underground ticket with the words: "I want this to become my ticket to the dreams". (9.5)

15. Manager whose final game at the helm was a 3-0 defeat to Aston Villa, a club he would take charge of the following season. (3.8)

Round 9 - Jimmy Greaves

The greatest goal scorer in the history of Tottenham Hotspur is Jimmy Greaves who racked up an incredible 266 goals in just 381 appearances. Further. he is the highest goal scorer in the history of the English top-flight with 357 goals. He won two FA Cups and a Cup Winners' Cup with Spurs as well as the World Cup with England and a Serie A title.

Across

2. Name of his autobiography written in 2003.

4. Greaves only career red card came in the 1962/63 Cup Winners' Cup semi final against OFK Beograd who were from this former nation.

7. He missed three months at the start of the 1965-66 season after being diagnosed with hepatitis, an inflammation of this organ.

8. Player that Greaves lost his place to in the 1966 World Cup after an injury in the group games. (5,5)

10. During a defeat to Brazil a stray dog ran onto the pitch and evaded all of the players' efforts to catch it until Greaves got down on all fours to beckon the animal. This legendary Brazil winger was so amused he took the dog home as a pet.

12. He was a team captain on this sporting quiz show opposite Andy Gray and Emlyn Hughes which aired from 1987-90. (8,9)

15. Club that Spurs finished second to in Greaves first season and that he scored twice against in the 1962 Charity Shield. (7,4)

16. Manager who signed him for Spurs. (4,9)

18. Club he started his career at and scored 132 goals in 169 games for.

20. After the departure of strike partner Bobby Smith to Brighton, Greaves struck up a new partnership with this new signing which he says was even more effective. (4,7)

Down

1. He received an MBE in the 2021 New Year Honours list, along with this fellow 1966 World Cup squad winner who were the last two members of the squad to be honoured by the Queen. (3,7)

3. He co-hosted a football talk show called Saint and Greavsie with this former Liverpool striker. (3,2,4)

5. Italian side Greaves signed for in 1961 for £80,000. (2,5)

6. Welshman who assisted Greaves first goal in the 1962/63 Cup Winners' Cup Final. (5,5)

9. He had scored 366 goals in the top five European leagues, a record that lasted until 2017 when it was finally surpassed by this man. (9,7)

11. He scored a hat-trick on his first team debut, including a flying scissor kick, in a 5-2 win over this Lancashire side.

13. Brian Clough, manager of this club at the time, tried to sign Greaves when he left Spurs but he wanted to stay in London. (5,6)

14. In 1963, Greaves became England's all-time leading goalscorer after overtaking Preston legend Sir Tom Finney and this Bolton one-club man. (3,9)

17. Newspaper he was a columnist for from 1979-2009. (3,3)

19. County he was born in.

Round 10 - Glenn Hoddle

One of the most gifted and creative English footballers of his generation. Glenn Hoddle dazzled the White Hart Lane faithful in his 12 seasons with the club. He scored an incredible 110 goals from midfield in 490 appearances and later returned to the club as manager in 2001.

Across

1. He made his farewell England cap against this former nation in 1988. (6.5)

3. Manager who he flourished under for most of his Spurs career. (5.10)

4. He scored a spectacular strike on his First Division debut past this England goalkeeper in 1976. (5.7)

7. Player he controversially omitted from his 1998 World Cup Squad whilst England manager. (4.9)

8. His final goal at the Lane came against this side after picking up the ball from inside his own hall before dribbling past three players and rounding the goalkeeper.

10. Club that Hoddle was manager of before Spurs.

13. Club he took over as manager in 2004 after leaving Spurs where he drew 34 of his 76 league games in charge. (13.9)

17. Hoddle was involved in the first ever Spurs team to lose an FA Cup Final which came against this side. (8.4)

18. Hoddle defeated this former club 5-1 in a League Cup semi-final as Spurs manager.

19. Club he earnt promotion to the Premier League with as player-manager. (7.4)

Down

1. Nation where his Glenn Hoddle Academy is based.

2. Club he scored for Spurs in a FA Cup Final and replay against. (6.4.7)

5. Legendary Spurs left-back who Hoddle came on for to make his first team debut. (5.7)

6. He helped Spurs to a 6-2 aggregate win over Feyenoord in 1983 and swapped shirts with this player after the match who had been dismissive of Hoddle's ability before the first leg. (5.6)

9. Manager who signed Hoddle for Monaco after he left Spurs. (6.6)

11. Spurs legend who was his idol growing up. (6.7)

12. His 490 Spurs appearances puts him 6th on the all-time appearance list. 39 ahead of this goalkeeper. (3.9)

14. Former Spurs player who was Hoddle's assistant when he was manager. (4.6)

15. Hoddle's teammate at Monaco who was the first African player to win the World Player of the Year and the Ballon d'Or. (6.4)

16. Side he scored a memorable goal against in 1983 when he Cruyff turned a player with his first touch before chipping the ball over the goalkeeper.

Spurs had a few grounds in their first six years before eventually settling behind a public house named the White Hart, a disused plant nursery. This would remain their home for the next 118 years before moving into the state-of-the-art 62,850-seater Tottenham Hotspur stadium, widely regarded as one of the best sports arenas on the planet.

Across

1. Spurs' application to take over this stadium as their new home was rejected in 2011. (7,7)

3. A statue of this former manager will be placed on the south west approach to the new stadium. (4,9)

6. Street that lied behind the biggest stand at White Hart Lane. (9,6)

7. The club's largest ever home league win of 9-0 came in 1977 against this West Country side. (7,6)

9. The design of the new South Stand was inspired by the 'yellow wall' from this team's stadium. (8,8)

10. The last goal at White Hart Lane was scored by this former England captain. (5,6)

12. Opponents for Spurs' first competitive game at the new stadium. (7,6)

13. Scored the winning goal in the first North London Derby at the new stadium. (4,12)

15. London borough that both stadiums were/are located.

16. Former player who made dents in the 4.5m high fibreglass replica of the Spurs cockerel after shooting at it with an air rifle. (4,9)

17. Alternative name of the South Stand. (4,4,3)

18. The highest attendance at White Hart Lane was 75,083 which came in a FA Cup tie against this North East side.

19. Name of the report published in 1990 after the Hillsborough disaster that mandated all-seater stadiums.

20. White Hart Lane was more often referred to as this by Spurs fans. (3,4)

Down

2. Spurs final game at White Hart Lane was a 2-1 win against this side. (10,6)

4. Famous architect that designed White Hart Lane and many other famous grounds around the UK. (9,6)

5. Californian team who won the first ever NFL match hosted at the Tottenham Hotspur Stadium after beating the Chicago Bears 24-21. (7,7)

8. First competitive goal scorer at the new stadium. (3,5,3)

11. The first ever game at White Hart Lane was a 4-1 win against this Nottinghamshire side. (5,6)

14. Name of the grade II listed house where the club's museum is located.

Round 12 - Academy Graduates

The Tottenham academy is renowned around the world for producing great talents. Can you name this select group of 20 players based on these clues?

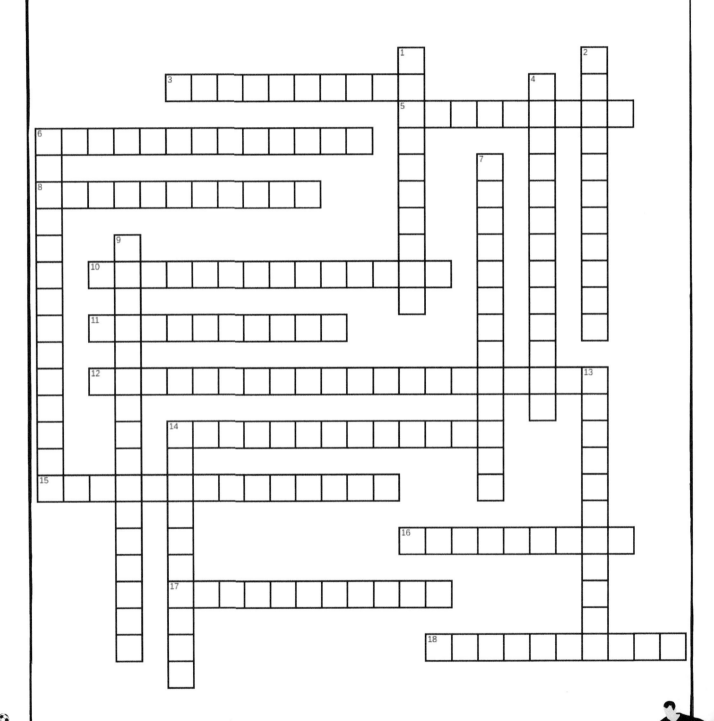

Across

3. Signed for Spurs from Arsenal who scored and set up two others in the 2009 League Cup semi-final first leg against Burnley. (5.5)

5. Became the youngest manager in Premier League history having been forced to retire due to a fractured skull. (4.5)

6. Loaned out seven times who is best known for his time at Hull City and West Brom. (4.9)

8. 6ft 7 in striker who holds the Premier League record for most headed goals. (5.6)

10. Right-back who made his Spurs debut in the same game as Tom Carroll and Harry Kane who went on to play for Fulham and West Ham. (4.10)

11. One-club man and former captain described by Harry Redknapp as "an absolute freak" for being able to play Premier League football despite not being able to train in the latter years of his career. (6.4)

12. USA international centre-back who has been loaned out six times including a spell with Bournemouth in 2020/21. (7.6.7)

14. Stiker who was loaned out eleven times between 2009 and 2014 before eventually leaving on a permanent deal to Swindon in 2017. (8.5)

15. Winger who had nine loan spells away from Spurs in his 7 years at the club and won the 2018/19 Premier League Goal of the Season. (6.8)

16. Three-time Premier League golden boot winner, World Cup golden boot winner and Spurs' second top goalscorer of all-time. (5.4)

17. Midfielder who helped Norwich to the Championship title in 2020/21 and made a combined 23 Premier League appearances for Spurs in the previous two seasons. (6.5)

18. Made over 100 Premier League appearances for Spurs in the early 90s who is one of nine players to score Premier League goals for six different clubs. (4.6)

Down

1. Lifelong Spurs fan widely praised for his performance against Real Madrid in 2017 in which he kept Luka Modrić and Toni Kroos at bay. (5.5)

2. Republic of Ireland international striker who has had loan spells with Millwall, Ipswich and MK Dons. (4.7)

4. Algerian midfielder who made 66 appearances for Spurs before spending time at Schalke and Newcastle. (5.8)

6. Won the Man of the Match for his performance against Manchester City on the opening matchday of the 2021/22 Premier League. (6.8)

7. Attacking midfielder who has made Premier League appearances for Spurs, West Brom and Huddersfield. (4.9)

9. Right-back who won man of the match on his Premier League debut against Newcastle in 2017 who was sold to Southampton for £12 million in 2020. (4.6.6)

13. Irish right-back who would make 272 appearances for the club before representing Newcastle and Birmingham. (7.4)

14. Joined Fulham as part of the £25 million deal to bring Ryan Sessegnon to the club. (4.6)

Round 13 - Club Captains

The club have had many legendary captains in their history. Can you name the last 20 based on their years as captain as well as the number of appearances and goals for the club?

Across

1. 1964-68 - 318 apps. 51 goals. (4.6)

3. 1956-57 - 260 apps. 7 goals. (4.6)

7. 1987 - 65 apps. 2 goals. (7.5)

8. 1954-55 - 250 apps. 24 goals. (3.6)

9. 2015-present - 374 apps. 0 goals and counting. (4.6)

11. 2003-05 - 49 apps. 4 goals. (5.8)

13. 1955-56 & 1959-64 - 382 apps. 29 goals. (5.12)

14. 1946-54 - 324 apps. 14 goals. (3.7)

16. 1975-86 - 866 apps. 39 goals. (5.8)

17. 2005-12 - 323 apps. 14 goals. (6.4)

18. 1987-98 - 619 apps. 27 goals. (4.6)

19. 1968-72 - 373 apps. 25 goals. (4.7)

20. 1986 - 330 apps. 0 goals. (3.8)

Down

2. 2014-15 - 140 apps. 9 goals. (6.6)

4. 2012-14 - 324 apps. 10 goals. (7.6)

5. 1958-59 - 317 apps. 208 goals. (5.5)

6. 1972-75 - 260 apps. 76 goals. (6.6)

10. 2001-03 - 277 apps. 124 goals. (5.10)

12. 1957-58 - 68 apps. 2 goals. (4.5)

15. 1998-2001 - 315 apps. 15 goals. (3.8)

Round 14 - Harry Kane

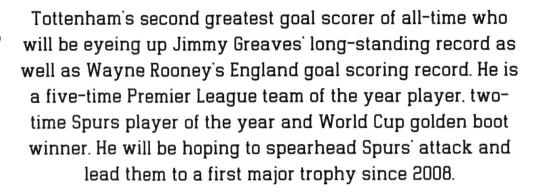

Tottenham's second greatest goal scorer of all-time who will be eyeing up Jimmy Greaves' long-standing record as well as Wayne Rooney's England goal scoring record. He is a five-time Premier League team of the year player, two-time Spurs player of the year and World Cup golden boot winner. He will be hoping to spearhead Spurs' attack and lead them to a first major trophy since 2008.

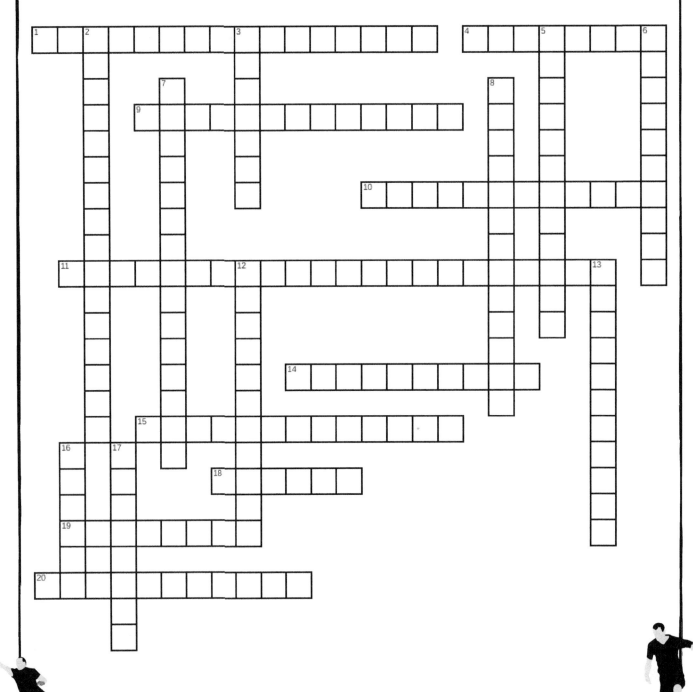

Across

1. Former Argentine striker who Pochettino compared Kane to in 2017. (7,9)

4. Club he won Young Player of the Season with in 2011/12.

9. Club that he scored four goals against in a Premier League game in 2017. (9,4)

10. Only two Englishmen have scored more Premier League hat tricks than Kane. Alan Shearer and this man. (6,6)

11. Club he scored a curling left footed shot from the edge of the box against shortly after being named on the New Years Honours list for an MBE. (13,9)

14. Player he overtook to become the highest goalscorer for Spurs in North London derby history. (5,5)

15. Name of his wife and childhood sweetheart. (5,8)

18. Kane scored his first professional hat-trick against Asteras Tripolis who are from this country.

19. Surname of the player who had the number 10 shirt for Spurs before Kane.

20. Greater London town he was born in.

Down

2. Club he scored against in the away leg of the 2018/19 round of 16 tie. (8,8)

3. Club he spent time as a youth player from 2001-02.

5. Former club he announced he'll sponsor to help them through the Covid-19 pandemic. (6,6)

6. Bulgarian side he scored his 200th Spurs goal against in his 300th appearance for the club during a 2021/21 Europa League group stage match.

7. Player he overtook in 2018 to become Spurs' top goalscorer in the Premier League era after scoring his 98th goal league goal for the club. (5,10)

8. Club he had a brief loan spell with in 2013 and scored 4 goals against in 2017. (9,4)

12. He scored his 100th Premier League goal after 141 games. only this player has reached this feat in fewer games. (4,7)

13. He assisted four goals for Son Heung-min and scored the other in a 5-2 away win against this side in 2020.

16. Country he scored a World Cup hat trick against.

17. Club he scored a goal from just inside the opposition half against in injury time to win a pre-season International Champions Cup game.

Round 15 - Gary Lineker & Paul Gascoigne

Gazza and Lineker formed a formidable partnership for Spurs in their three seasons together from 1989 to 1992 scoring 113 goals between them. Their highlights in the Spurs shirt came in the 1991 FA Cup run when both starred in the semi-final victory to fire Spurs to their first final in 9 years.

Across

3. Gazza ruptured his own cruciate ligament after a bad tackle on this Nottingham Forest player in the 1991 FA Cup Final. (4.7)

6. Manager that Gazza and Lineker played under at Spurs. (5.8)

8. Gascoigne scored a late winner against this then Division Two side to send Spurs into the FA Cup semi-final. (5.6)

11. Manager who tried to sign Lineker so he could partner his ex-teammate Mark Hughes up front but he chose to join Spurs instead. (4.8)

12. Side that Gazza was sold to due to the £10 million debt that Spurs had at the time.

13. Lineker scored a hat trick in one of his first games at the Lane against this London side. (6.4.7)

16. "That is schoolboys' own stuff." famously remarked by this commentator after Gazza scored a 30-yard free kick in a FA Cup semi-final (5.6)

17. Snack company that Lineker has appeared in television advertisements.

18. Japanese club that Lineker joined for £2 million from Spurs. (6.7)

19. Lineker scored the second quickest World Cup hat trick of all-time in 1986 against this Eastern European side.

20. Club that Spurs signed Lineker from.

Down

1. East Midlands side that Gazza scored a hat-trick against in September 1990 in a 3-0 home win. (5.6)

2. London club that Lineker scored a hat-trick against in April 1992. one of his final appearances at the Lane. (4.3.6)

4. Club that Gazza supported as a boy and was signed by Spurs from. (9.6)

5. Club other than Spurs that Lineker and Gazza played for.

7. Lineker and Gazza starred together at World Cup '90 hosted in this country.

9. Lineker scored on his final appearance for Spurs and his last ever goal in English football at this stadium. (3.8)

10. Club that Lineker supported as a boy and started his career at. (9.4)

14. Lineker won the Football Writers' Association Footballer of the Year in 1991/92 and was the first Spurs player to win it since this player in 1986/87. (5.5)

15. Side who Lineker scored a brace against in the 1991 FA Cup semi-final.

Round 16 - Luka Modrić & Gareth Bale

Two modern icons who played alongside each other for four seasons at Spurs and another eight at Real Madrid. They eventually outgrew the team but were firm fan favourites during their time and will be fondly remembered. They commanded fees of nearly £120 million from Madrid where they went on to win an incredible four Champions Leagues in five years.

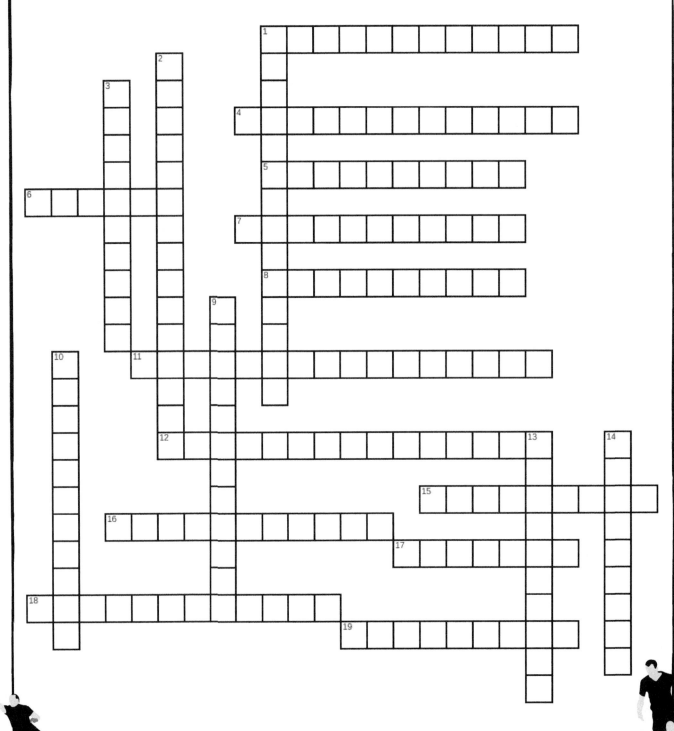

Across

1. Premier League manager who said that Modrić should have won the 2010/11 Player of the Season award. (4,8)

4. Club that Bale scored a long-range dipping strike from over 30 yards against in the dying stages of the game to secure the win in February 2013. (4,3,6)

5. Opposition that Bale scored a Champions League hat-trick against which burst him on to the world scene. (5,5)

6. For the 2012/13 season. Bale requested a new number higher than three as he "wasn't a left-back anymore" and received this number.

7. Club that Spurs signed Bale from in 2007.

8. Bale scored his first Premier League hat-trick against this side on Boxing Day 2012. (5,5)

11. Bale became only the second player after this man to win the PFA Players' Player of the Year. PFA Young Player of the Year and FWA Footballer of the Year in the same season. (9,7)

12. Bale scored a hat-trick against this side in May 2021 during his return loan spell to the club. (9,6)

15. Modrić scored his first goal of the 2011/12 season with a 25-yarder against this side in a 4-0 win at White Hart Lane.

16. Modrić chose the number 14 shirt at Spurs. later recalling that he wore it in honour of this player. (5,6)

17. Club who relentlessly pursued Modrić's signature in the summer of 2011 and had three bids turned down including one for £40 million on deadline day.

18. Former Spurs manager who signed Modrić for Real Madrid. (4,8)

19. In December 2011 Bale scored away at Bolton and proceeded to take off his left boot with had stitched on it "RIP _____" after this fellow countryman had recently passed away. (4,5)

Down

1. Side who Bale and Modrić won two of their four Champions League Finals against with Real Madrid. (8,6)

2. Modrić's last goal was a powerful 25-yard volley against this side in May 2012. (6,9)

3. Former Premier League and Australia striker who is Modrić's cousin. (4,6)

9. Modrić was labelled as a lightweight for the Premier League by sections of the media in his early days at Spurs. as well as this rival manager. (6,6)

10. Manager who signed Modrić for Spurs. (6,5)

13. Spurs paid £16.5 million for Modrić which was a joint club record with this player. (6,4)

14. Opposition that Bale scored a head high volley against into the top corner of the goal in 2010. (5,4)

Round 17 - Hugo Lloris & Son Heung-min

Two loyal servants who have appeared over 650 times combined for the club with Son scoring over 100 goals and Lloris becoming the first player to make 300 Premier League appearances for Spurs.

Across

1. Son's national team. (5,5)

4. Military force that Son trained for his mandatory service with during the 2020 Covid-19 pandemic. (6,5)

5. Lloris won his 100th international cap in a World Cup match against this South American opposition.

7. Monaco striker that Lloris saved a penalty from in a 2016 Champions League match. (7,6)

9. Son became the highest scoring Asian in Champions League history when he overtook this former Dynamo Kiev and Uzbekistan striker. (6,9)

10. Club that Spurs signed Son Heung-min from. (5,10)

12. Manager who signed Lloris for Spurs. (5,6,4)

14. Lloris' Spurs debut ended this goalkeeper's run of 310 consecutive games in the Premier League. (4,7)

15. Lloris's city of birth and first club.

18. Manchester City player that Lloris saved a penalty from in a 2019 Champions League match. (6,6)

19. The €30m transfer fee paid by Spurs broke the transfer record for an Asian held since 2001 by this Japanese legend. (9,6)

20. Son won the 2020 Puskas award and 2019/20 Premier League goal of the season with an individual effort against this side.

Down

2. German club that Son joined as a 16-year-old from South Korea and played for until 2013.

3. National team that Lloris captained to World Cup glory.

6. Lloris made a spectacular one-handed stop on the goal-line to deny this Mexican striker in a 2016 Champions League game against Bayer Leverkusen. (6,9)

8. He overtook this player to become the Premier Leagues highest scoring Asian of all-time in 2017. (4,2,4)

11. Son scored a Champions League quarter-final brace against this side. (10,4)

13. Son's first Premier League hat-trick came against this side.

16. Club Lloris was signed from.

17. London side that Son scored his first Spurs hat-trick against in a FA Cup tie.

You've done well to reach this point: I hope you have learned lots of cool facts about the Lilywhites. Here are three rounds of general questions from a range of categories to finish off. Good luck!

Across

2. Strange loan signing made from First Division Sheffield Wednesday in 2001 who would only make four appearances in the season before spending eight years at Huddersfield in the lower leagues. (4,5)

4. South African centre-back signed after an impressive 2010 World Cup. (7,7)

6. Spurs' club record defeat of 8-0 came against this German side in the Intertoto Cup in 1995.

8. Argentina legend who once pulled on the Spurs number 10 shirt in a testimonial game in honour of his international teammate Ossie Ardiles. (5,8)

10. 16-year-old wonderkid signed in controversial fashion from Crystal Palace who would only make four appearances for Spurs before being released in 2013. (4,7)

11. Striker who scored a long-range brace against Birmingham City in 2011 to earn the club a spot in the Europa League. (5,12)

14. Eighth-tier side that Spurs beat 5-0 in the 4th round of the 2020/21 FA Cup.

17. Striker who scored the Premier League's 10,000th ever goal in a game for Spurs against Fulham in 2001. (3,9)

18. Spurs' oldest first team player was this goalkeeper at the age of 42 years 176 days in 2013. (4,7)

19. Spurs' record Premier League away win of 7-1 came against this side in 2017. (4,4)

20. First Finnish player to play for Spurs. (5,6)

Down

1. Journeyman goalkeeper that had a short spell with Spurs who became the first to save a penalty in a FA Cup Final and the first to captain his side to victory since 1875 when he did so with Wimbledon In 1988. (4,7)

3. Spurs collected at least one major trophy in each of the six decades from the 1950s to 2000s – an achievement only matched by this side. (10,6)

5. Kit manufacturer from 2012-17. (5,6)

7. Norwegian goalkeeper who was the first ever substitute in the Premier League after he came on for the injured Ian Walker for Spurs. (4,10)

9. Ledley King's shirt number during his time at Spurs. (6,3)

12. Scored a thumping 30-yard strike at the Kop End in October 2019. (6,7)

13. Canadian right-back who spent three seasons at Spurs and made 33 league appearances in the 2005/06 season. (4,8)

15. Serie A and three-time UEFA Cup winner with Inter Milan who also played in the 1994 World Cup Final and joined Spurs in 1998 before leaving a year later. (6,5)

16. Goalkeeper Paul Robinson scored an 80 meter free-kick against this side.

Across

2. Midfielder signed from Newcastle in 2005 who went on to make 202 appearances for the club scoring 26 goals. (8.5)

4. Only Frenchman in Spurs' Hall of Fame and to win the Player or the Year award. (5.6)

6. Author of the Harry Potter series who is a Spurs fan. (1.1.7)

9. Spurs' record signing. (6.8)

10. Shirt sponsor from 1983-95 & 1999-2002.

11. Welshman signed from Third Division Peterborough United in 2000 who won the Spurs player of the season award in 2002. (5.6)

14. Dutch midfielder who scored four Premier League goals against Arsenal in his time with the club. (6.3.3.5)

16. Club that Serge Aurier and Lucas Moura were signed from. (5.5.7)

17. Opponents who Spurs have faced most often in European competition with 8.

18. Scored a 94th minute equaliser against Arsenal in a 4-4 draw at the Emirates in 2008. (5.6)

19. 2011/12 Player of the Season. (5.6)

Down

1. Player signed from Seville in part-exchange for Erik Lamela in 2021. (5.3)

2. First non-British player to win Spurs' top goal scorer award. (6.9)

3. Scored a brace for Spurs in the first North London derby in the Premier League era. (4.6)

5. Left-back and local community presence who said in 2011 that he plays football for the money rather than the intrinsic pleasure of the game. (6.5.6)

7. Goalkeeper who has made the most appearances for Spurs. (3.8)

8. Striker signed for a club record £4.5 million from Crystal Palace who scored Spurs' first goal of the new millennium. (5.9)

12. Centre-back sold to Stoke City for £18 million in 2017. (5.6)

13. Irish right-back who made 44 appearances for Spurs between 2002 and 2006. (7.5)

15. Singer born in Tottenham who is one of the world's best-selling music artists. with sales of over 120 million records and is a big Spurs fan.

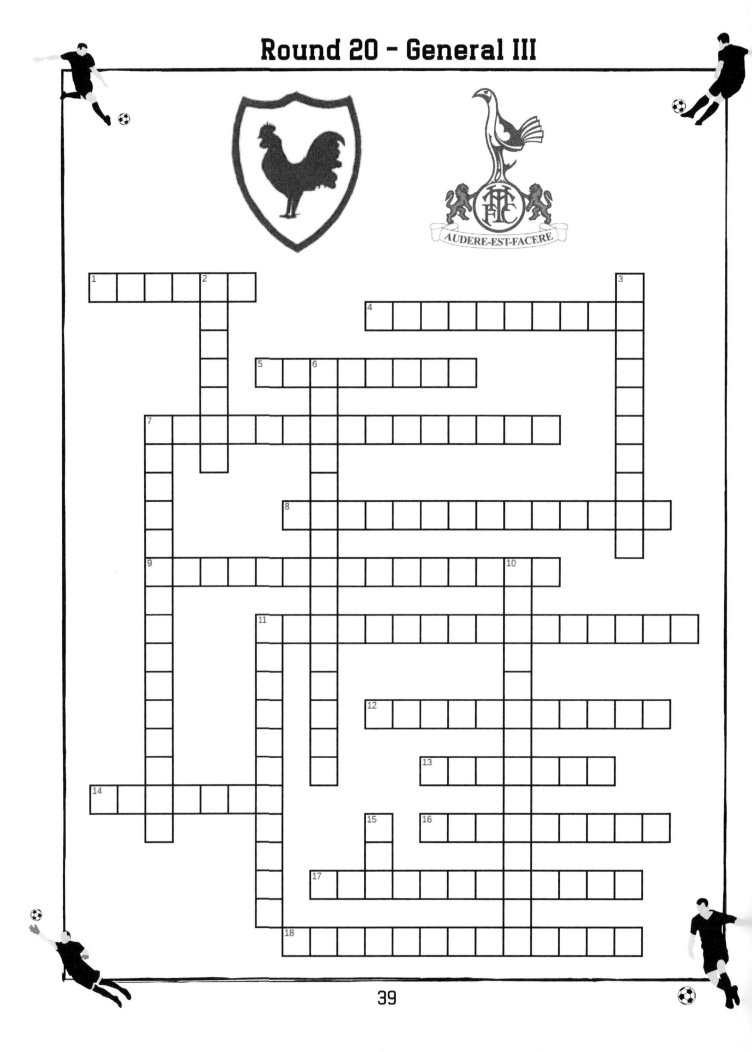

Across

1. Spurs' first ever European match came in 1961 when they played Górnik Zabrze from this country in the Cup Winners' Cup.

4. Highest fee ever received by Spurs for an Englishman was for this player. (4.6)

5. The club's emblem.

7. Scored the equaliser in normal time against Chelsea in the 2008 League Cup Final. (7.8)

8. Scotsman who formed a formidable strike partnership with Garth Crooks in the 1980s. (5.9)

9. Eventual winners who knocked Spurs out of the last ever UEFA Cup campaign before it was rebranded as the Europa League. (8.7)

11. Dane who scored 69 goals in 305 appearances for the club and is a two-time Player of the Year. (9.7)

12. The decision to host an England international against this side in 1935 led to protests from the Jewish supporters of the club. (4.7)

13. Their training ground is on Hotspur Way in Bulls Cross in this London Borough.

14. Spurs faced this side in the first ever all-London FA Cup Final.

16. Side that Spurs defeated in a 1995 FA Cup 6th Round tie despite having a poor record at their ground.

17. The club's motto. (2.4.2.2.2)

18. Defender named in the 2012/13 and 2017/18 PFA Team of the Year. (3.10)

Down

2. Spanish ground that Spurs secured a 1-1 draw in the 2019/19 Champions League group stage. (3.4)

3. Scored a 'rabona' against Arsenal. (4.6)

6. Number 4 for the 2021/22 season. (9.6)

7. Spurs' first £40 million player. (8.7)

10. Norwegian who was top scorer in the 1998/99 and 1999/2000 seasons. (7.7)

11. Former Spurs player who is the only man to represent England whilst playing for a French club. (5.6)

15. Word associated with Spurs fans which was used by opposition fans in the 60s as an anti-semitic insult but has now been fully embraced by fans.

Answers

Round 2 - 1950/60s

1. JOHNWHITE
2. TERRYVENABLES
3. DANNYBLANCHFLOWER
4. MARTINCHIVERS
5. MANCHESTERCITY
6. BOBBYSMITH
7. BURNLEY
8. CLIFFJONES
9. BILLNICHOLSON
10. JIMMYGREAVES
11. LENDUQUEMIN
12. ATLETICOMADRID
13. SHEFFIELDWEDNESDAY
14. LEICESTERCITY
15. TERRYDYSON
16. PUSHANDRUN
17. CREWEALEXANDRA
18. CHELSEA
19. ALANGILZEAN
20. DAVEMACKAY

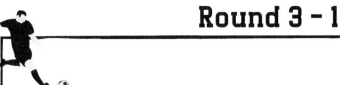

A crossword puzzle grid with the following answers:

Across:
- STEVE PERRYMAN
- RALPH COATES
- MARTIN PETERS
- WOLVERHAMPTON WANDERERS
- DAVID PLEAT
- IRVING SCHOLAR
- ALAN MULLERY
- MONACO
- OSSIE ARDILES
- CLIVE ALLEN

Down:
- GARY LINEKER
- PAUL GASCOIGNE
- TONY PARKS
- STONY PARKS
- KEITH BURKINSHAW
- TERRY NEIL
- PAT JENNINGS
- ASTON VILLA
- ALEX FERGUSON
- GLENN HODDLE
- RICKY VILLA

Round 4 – 1990s

Across

3. DAVID GINOLA
5. PAUL GASCOIGNE
6. BARNSLEY
9. OSSIE ARDILES
13. NOTTINGHAM FOREST
15. ALLAN NIELSEN
16. ALAN SUGAR
17. DENNIS BERGKAMP
18. LEICESTER CITY
19. GEORGE GRAHAM

Down

1. JAPAN
2. TEDDY SHERINGHAM
4. JURGEN KLINSMANN
7. LES FERDINAND
8. PAT VAN DEN HAUW
10. CHRISTIAN GROSS
11. STEFFEN FREUND
12. ROMANIA
14. TIM SHERWOOD

Round 5 - 2000s

Across

1. JERMAINDEFOE
4. WESTHAMUNITED
6. SOLCAMPBELL
9. JACQUESSANTINI
10. JONATHANWOODGATE
13. EDGARDAVIDS
17. LEDLEYKING
19. GUSPOYET
20. DANIELLEVY

Down

2. DIMITARBERBATOV
3. LUKAMODRIC
5. SERGEIREBROV
7. CHELSEA
8. ROBBIEKEAN
11. HARRYREDKNAPP
12. READING
14. SOUTHAMPTON
15. MARTINJOL
16. DARRENBENT
18. DAVIDBENTLEY

Round 6 - 2010s

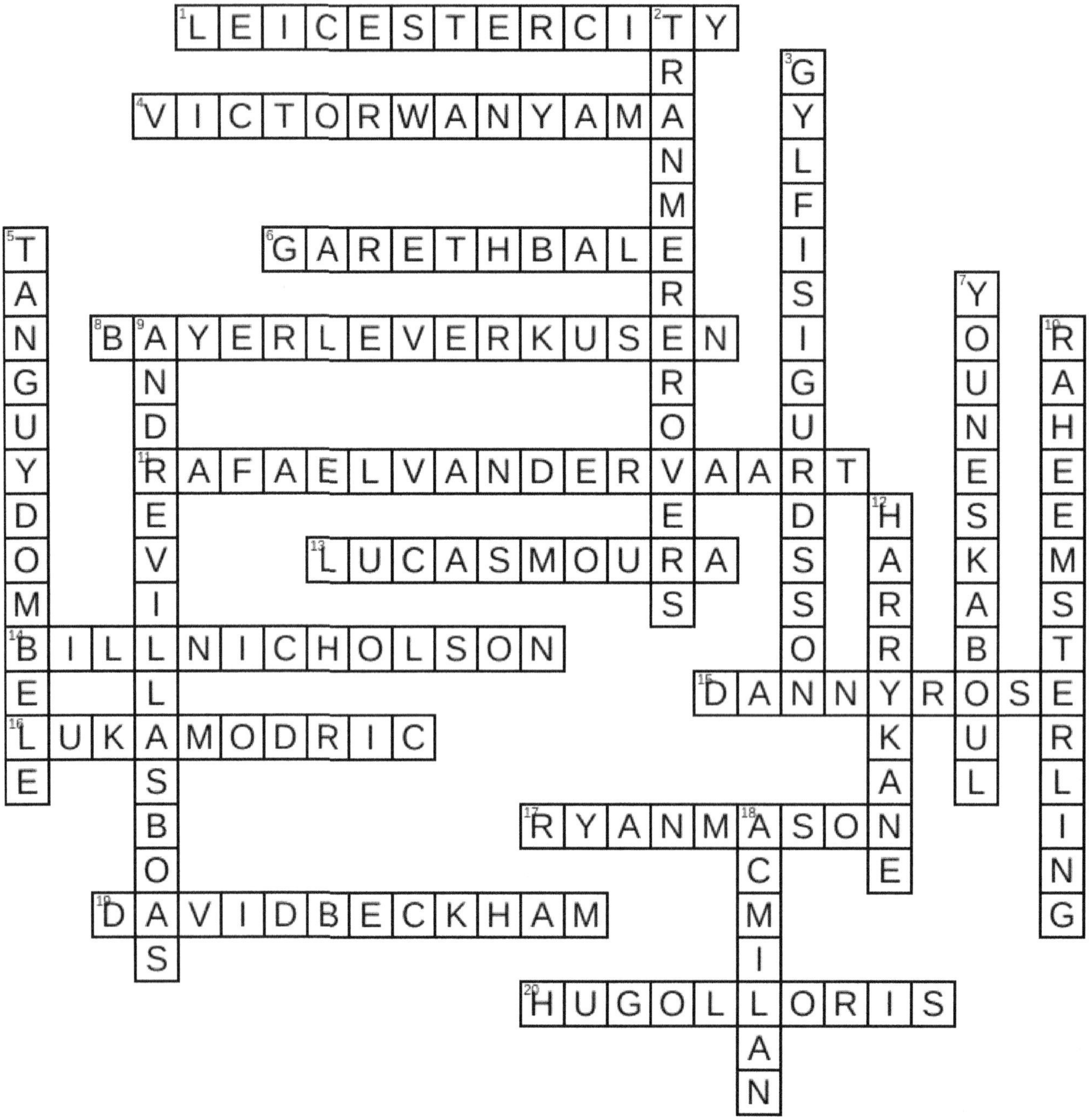
1 LEICESTERCITY
2 TRANMEREROVERS
3 GYLFISIGURDSSON
4 VICTORWANYAMA
5 TANGUYDOMBELE
6 GARETHBALE
7 YOUNESKABOUL
8 BAYERLEVERKUSEN
9 ANDREVILLASBOAS
10 RAHEEMSTERLING
11 RAFAELVANDERVAART
12 HARRYKANE
13 LUCASMOURA
14 BILLNICHOLSON
15 DANNYROSE
16 LUKAMODRIC
17 RYANMASON
18 ACMILLAN
19 DAVIDBECKHAM
20 HUGOLLORIS

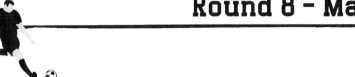

Round 8 - Managers

1 TERRYVENABLES

2 JOHNCAMERON

3 MARTINJOL

4 STEVEPERRYMAN

5 JUANDERAMOS

6 ANDREVILLASBOAS

7 JACQUESSANTINI

8 JIMMYANDERSON

9 PETERMCWILLIAM

10 HARRYREDKNAPP

11 OSSIEARDILES

12 CHRISTIANGROSS

13 RYANMASON

14 MAURICIOPOCHETTINO

15 TIMSHERWOOD

16 DAVIDPLEAT

17 GEORGEGRAHAM

18 JOSEMOURINHO

19 GLENNHODDLE

20 PETERSHREEVES

Round 9 - Jimmy Greaves

A crossword puzzle with the following answers:

Across:
2. GREAVSIE
4. YUGOSLAVIA
7. LIVER
8. GEOFFHURST
10. GARRINCHA
12. SPORTINGTRIANGLES
15. IPSWICHTOWN
16. BILLNICHOLSON
18. CHELSEA
20. ALANGILZEAN

Down:
1. RONFLOWERS
3. IANSTJOHN
5. ACMILAN
6. CLIFFJONES
9. CRISTIANORONALDO
11. BLACKPOOL
13. DERBYCOUNTY
14. NATLOFTHOUSE
17. THESUN
19. ESSEX

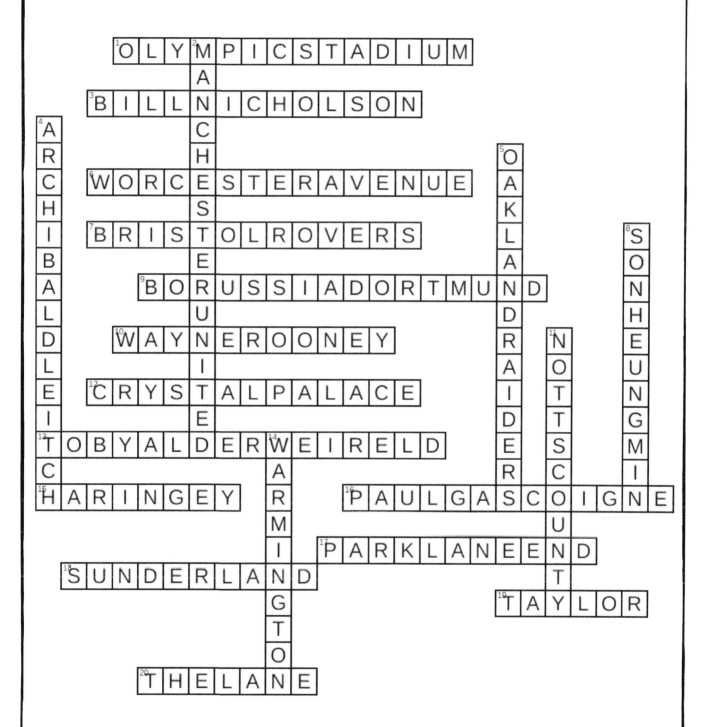

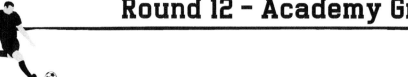

Round 12 - Academy Graduates

1. HARRYWINKS
2. TROYPARROTT
3. JAMIEOHARA
4. NABILBENTALEB
5. RYANMASON
6. JAKELIVERMORE
6. JAPHETTANGANGA
7. ALEXPRITCHARD
8. PETERCROUCH
9. KYLEWALKERPETERS
10. RYANFREDERICKS
11. LEDLEYKING
12. CAMERONCARTERVICKERS
13. STEPHENCARR
14. JONATHANOBIKA
14. JOSHONOMAH
15. ANDROSTOWNSEND
16. HARRYKANE
17. OLIVERSKIPP
18. NICKBARMBY

Round 13 - Club Captains

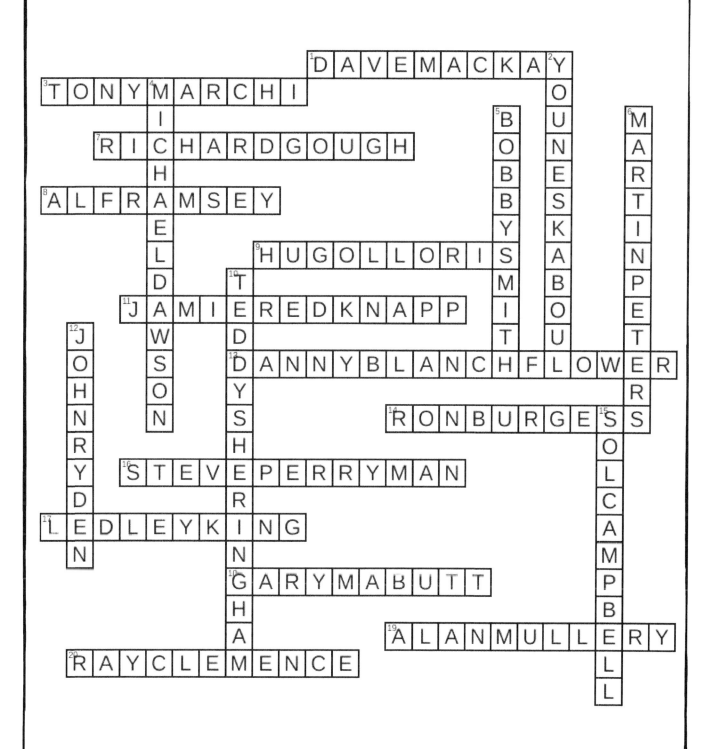

A crossword puzzle with the following filled answers:

1 Across: GABRIELBATISTUTA
4 Across: MILLWALL
9 Across: LEICESTERCITY
10 Across: ROBBIEFOWLER
11 Across: WOLVERHAMPTONWANDERERS
14 Across: BOBBYSMITH
15 Across: KATIEGOODLAND
18 Across: GREECE
19 Across: ADEBAYOR
20 Across: WALTHAMSTOW

Down answers include:
2 Down: BORUSSIADORTMUND
3 Down: ARSENAL
5 Down: LEYTONORIENT
6 Down: LUDOGORETS
7 Down: TEDDYSHERINGHAM
8 Down: LEICESTERCITY
12 Down: ALANSHEARER
13 Down: SOUTHAMPTON
16 Down: PANAMA
17 Down: JUVENTUS

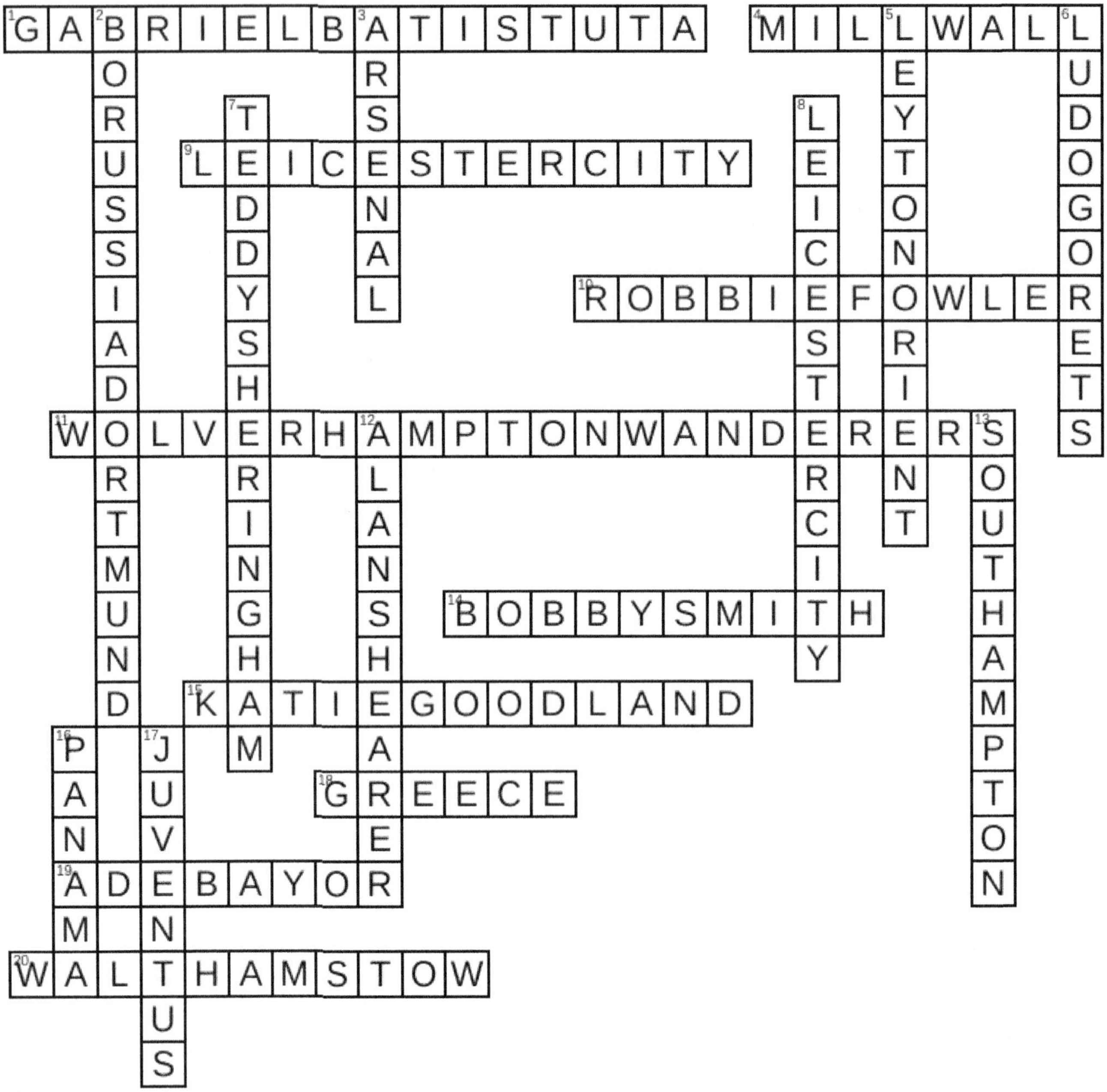

1. ALEXFERGUSON
2. BOLTONWANDERE
3. MARKVIDUKA
4. WESTHAMUNITED
5. INTERMILAN
6. ELEVEN
7. SOUTHAMPTON
8. ASTONVILLA
9. ARSENEWENGER
10. JUANDERAMOS
11. CRISTIANORONALDO
12. SHEFFIELDUNITED
13. DARRENBENT
14. STOKECITY
15. LIVERPOOL
16. JOHANCRUYFF
17. CHELSEA
18. JOSEMOURINHO
19. GARYSPEED

ATLETICOMADRID

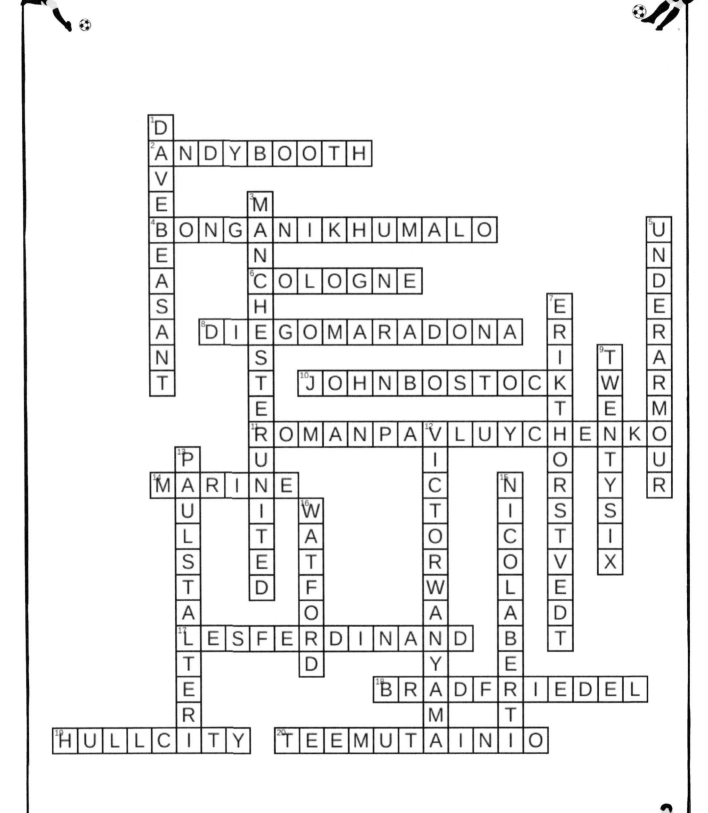

Crossword grid answers:

2 Across: ANDYBOOTH
4 Across: BONGANIKHUMALO
6 Across: COLOGNE
8 Across: DIEGOMARADONA
10 Across: JOHNBOSTOCK
11 Across: ROMANPAVLUYCHENKO
14 Across: MARINE
17 Across: LESFERDINAND
18 Across: BRADFRIEDEL
19 Across: HULLCITY
20 Across: TEEMUTAINIO

1 Down: DAVEBEASANT
3 Down: MANCHESTERUNITED
5 Down: UNDERARMOUR
7 Down: ERIKTHORSTVEDT
9 Down: TWENTYSIX
12 Down: VICTORWANYAMA
13 Down: PAULSTALTER
15 Down: NICOLALBERT
16 Down: WATFORD

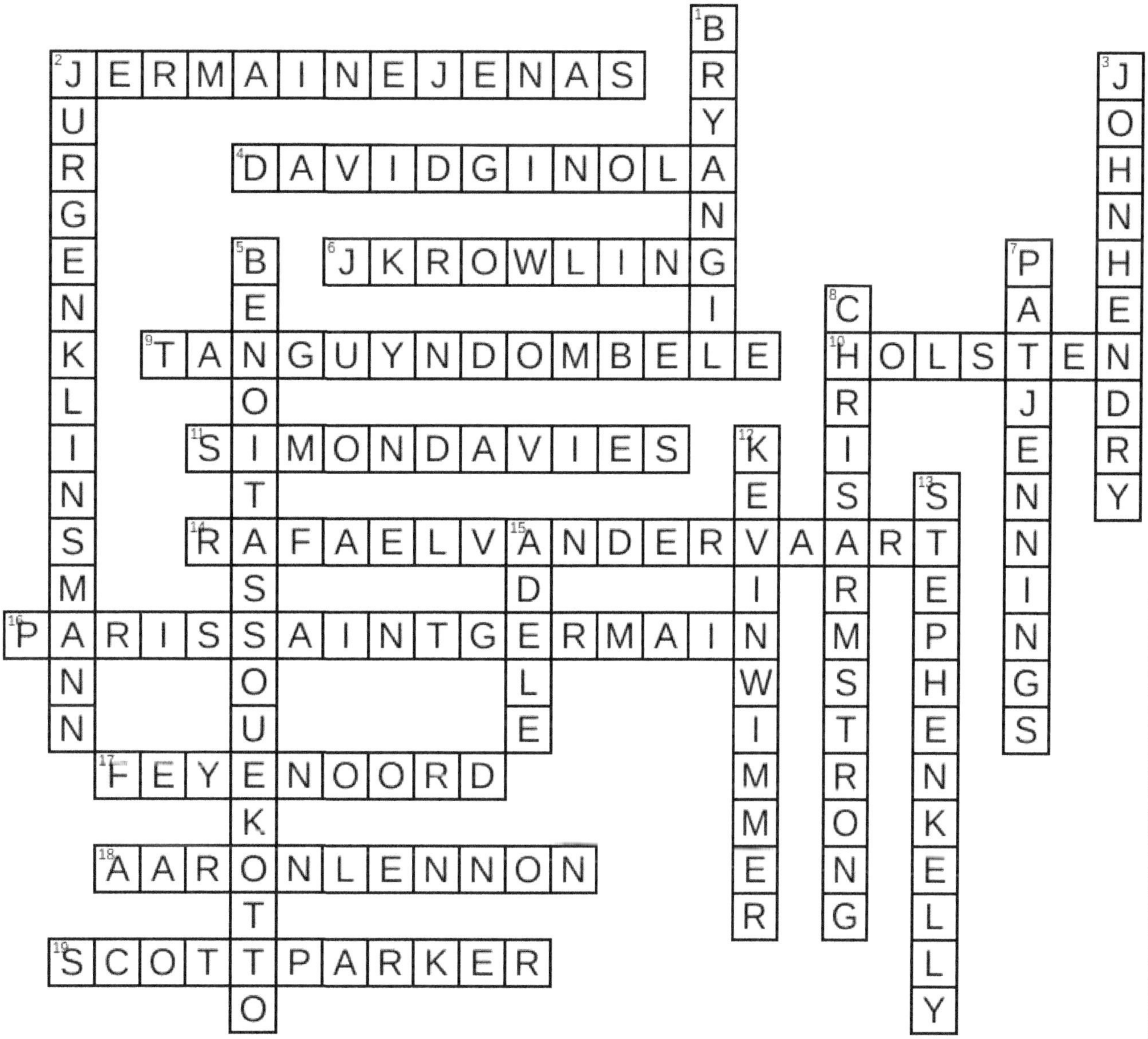
1 BRYANGIL
2 JERMAINEJENAS
2 JURGENKLINSMANN
3 JOHNHENDRY
4 DAVIDGINOLA
5 BENOITASSOUEKOTTO
6 JKROWLING
7 PATJENNINGS
8 CHRISARMSTRONG
9 TANGUYNDOMBELE
10 HOLSTEN
11 SIMONDAVIES
12 KEVINWIMMER
13 STEPHENKELLY
14 RAFAELVANDERVAART
15 ADELE
16 PARISSAINTGERMAIN
17 FEYENOORD
18 AARONLENNON
19 SCOTTPARKER

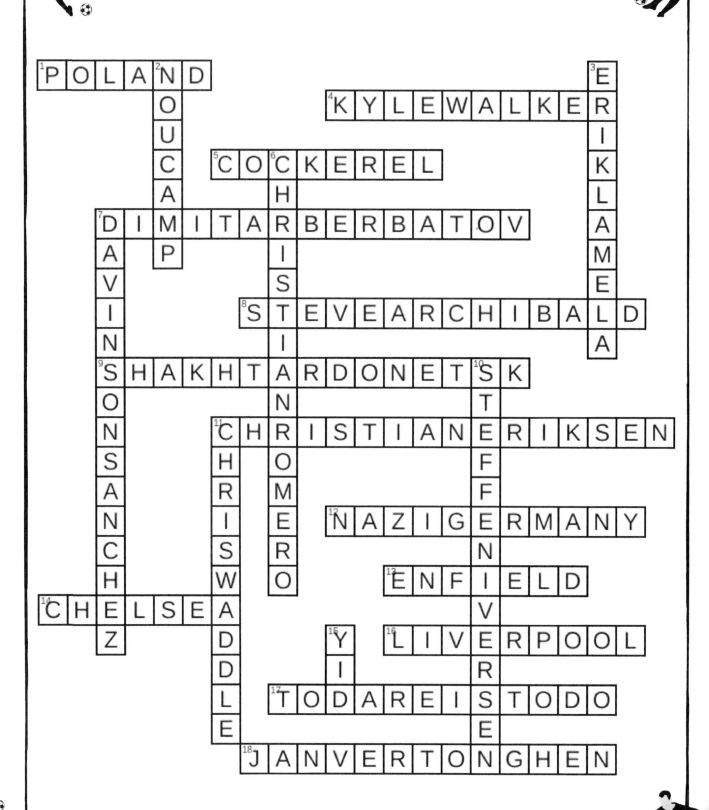

That's all folks, thank you so much for purchasing this Spurs crossword book. I really hope you enjoyed it and learnt some cool facts about the club to impress your fellow Lilywhites.

As a small independent publisher any reviews you can leave will be a big help as I try to grow my company and produce better and better books for you to enjoy.

If you have any criticisms, please do email me before leaving a negative review and I'd be happy to assist you if you have any problems!

kieran.brown2402@gmail.com

Printed in Great Britain
by Amazon

30495127R00037